When it Works
it feels like play

By the same author:

(as Tessa Stiven)
Poetry of Persons (1976)
While it is Yet Day (1977)

(as Tessa Ransford)
Light of the Mind (1980)
Fools and Angels (1984)
Shadows from the Greater Hill (1987)
A Dancing Innocence (1988)
Seven Valleys (1991)
Medusa Dozen (1994)
Scottish Selection (1998)

TESSA RANSFORD

When it Works it feels like play

THE RAMSAY HEAD PRESS
EDINBURGH

For my five grandchildren

Acknowledgements

Acknowledgements are due to the editors and publishers
of the following magazines in which some of the poems
in this volume have previously appeared:

After the Watergaw (anthology), *Asheville Poetry Review,*
Broadsheet (Inverness), *Chapman, Edinburgh Review, Fife Lines,*
The Interpreter's House, Lines Review, Present Poets (anthology),
Orte (Switzerland), *Remembered Place* (The Housman Society),
The Scotsman, Skinklin Star, West Coast Magazine, Zed₂O

Cover

Etching by Peter Standen

ISBN 1 873921 05 5

First published in 1998 by
The Ramsay Head Press
15 Gloucester Place
Edinburgh EH3 6EE

The publisher acknowledges the Financial assistance of
The Derick Bolton Poetry Trust

Printed in Scotland by Bell & Bain Limited, Glasgow

Contents

4 *Interpretive*

5 *Relative*

1 Meditative

The Shepherd of Remedello

*(The prehistoric man found at Hauslabjoch
the Otztal Alps on 19th September 1991)*

He went to sleep for five thousand years
not expecting a resurrection

high on the ridge where he tended flocks
with grass-woven cloak and birch tinderbox

copper axe and flintstone dagger
bow and quiver and hazel pannier.

Did he lose the track with goats and sheep
or cross the alps in search of help

over the mountains he knew from danger
traversing the heights as farmer-hunter?

His tribe and family in Val Venosta
stitched his garments from fur and feather.

He was climbing the pass as messenger
but with broken ribs and failing breath

could strain no further in dark and blizzard.
He nicely placed his tools and weapons

lay on his side with outstretched hands
to fall asleep in deepening cold.

Shrouded in ice he was never revealed
the glacier entombed him agelessly

preserved his face and limbs and clothes
frozen for ever just as he was:

an ancestral wonder, a Shepherd-Lord
Behold the Man Who Never Died.

Wondrous Child, Wounded Child

Up pony! Off we go on the long life-journey
from east to west like the sun,
bundled together, hoof-beat, heart-beat,
wheels cannot stop nor the pony slow down.

Proud boy, seven years old, holding the reins:
"Gee up, gee up!" you shout and already whoop
to the bumps and jolts of the dusty road,
and keeping the pony straight, trit trot,
guided round corners, the tug of the bit
and the huge spoke-wheels creak-creaking.

Five-year-old girl, you fold back into
your mother's right arm with a puzzled look,
apprehensive: will it cause us harm?
"Whoa! Whoa!" a little voice inside cries.
"Don't toss me about, I might fall out."

The *sais* stands by impassive and stares ahead.
It is in the hands of fate once
the pony is groomed and harnessed,
the trap cleaned and oiled.

Three in the pony trap, still, in the Nilgri Hills,
blue hills, dream hills, cool hills of India.

sais is the Hindi word for groom.

Legohead

Can't you see twigs at your fingers
branches, sticks at your feet?

Don't you sense the tree that you are,
processed from sunlight
and deep earthmould
but broken, scrappy, uprooted?

Don't you know you are bound
together artificially,
a temporary arrangement of dancing
cells and festive energy patterns?

You are yourself only
for this one exhibition,
then you will be dismantled and
your component parts will exist
in uncreated orders
of the seething universe
until some other form is built out of you.

You can't examine the little plastic bricks
that fit together your brain.
What an odd construction you are,
trying to be human, pretending,
Legohead!

Metaphysics

This birth is a planetary affair
since nothing worldly is a fraction worth
this present incarnation upon earth
and into our safe-keeping now and here.

His mother, weakened by her valiant strength
in labour, now shall never lose or lack
the love he needs; his cries, his very breath
of steady life her food, as she gives suck.

Weak is with strong alternately translated
from love to love in love by love created.

Extremities

How can a child be "guardian spirit"
to a grown man or woman? Novalis
found in twelve-year-old Sophie
that bewildering power, even as she,
on ripening, shrivelled into death.

Shelley called such beauty intellectual.
When I be-hold this baby boy and
perceive his grasp of colour, his
response to sound, his dance in
every limb while lying helpless

and his direct, wordless conversations
with his mother, I touch an immortality
more sacred than the hidden, fiery Ark,
transparent than Keats "writ in water."
I turn again to find this in the old

as they, also immobile, stored with
years of living, transform. themselves
once more into the seeming-empty
pure invisibility of love, in which
the smile, expression, person has to be.

Meditation

I sit beside Lord Buddha in the plane.
He keeps his balanced pose
upright, and can sleep there,
hands in the lotus position,
eyes never entirely shut
or entirely open.
Sometimes, very quietly,
he smokes a cigarette.

We travel side by side
through nights and days
and over arctic mountains,
seas and plains,
a lantern on the wingtip and
another on the tail, marking
the circle of this meditation space.

I endure my aching body
eyes shut or open, light on or off,
while Lord Buddha sits serene and
seems to gather strength
like mossy stones.

Continue now, and breathe a little longer:
there will be ripples in the lake:
it is a waterfall—a waterlily.

The Lightest Snow

Flake by separate snow-flake falls
Over Tintern Abbey, glades
between columns, arches, open
full moon ring of eastern window,
chimney places, staircases,
meadows spreading to the Wye
as it loops and lingers beneath
wooded hills, takes on snow.

Day is brief before the winter dark
returns. Flakes, like grace, are lit
by low pale cold sunbeams.
We are not warmed but awed by
beauty so austere. Yet the poem tells:
you will recall acts of kindness,
be captivated by a presence
never to be recaptured.
                              A deep coldness.
A winter day. The lightest snow.

The Real Thing

He had practised the turns and techniques
and taught his muscles to master the movements
until his body instinctively carried him safely
at high speed in the true direction
and stopped at once on command.

All this had happened slowly
after many a slog in unsympathetic winds
and unexhilarating falls,
with always the confinement of keeping
to the strip of spiked nylon that scars the slope.

*   *   *

One day he went up early:
The hill was alight in the dawn
deep-robed in delicate snow
smooth expansive and yielding
tempting to be tested by the long, curved skis.

Never did beaked ship setting sail on the Aegean
so cleave the succulent waters
with her long curved timbers
 in a favourable wind....
Never did Spitfire so dance the moving heavens
cascading into clouds
with a shout of breaking sunbeams
and in effortless speed....
Never did planet so penetrate the cosmos
in a whirlwheel of particles
that gravitate around her
to concentrate their shape....

Never did boy so lay-aside the substitute
set free his body to float in the universe
extended to the limit of its own perfect laws,
so control in a moment the infinity of movement
and know with a shout its effortless speed,
so curve through the contours of another dimension
and make his own mark
on the surface of the Real.

Blake's Wife

My love walked in a wild domain
I followed him as best I could
beyond the boundaries of the brain
half credible, half understood.
He hardly slept, strange music played
he wrote, dreamed, painted.

In love I pitied, helped him work
on copper plates, the ink and fire.
We cooled it down in printed books
of prophecy or soul's desire.
"The lark an angel on the wing"
purest line engraving.

His *spectre* visited for days
and silent brooded on the house.
I waited, made his soup, his clothes
until he found a form in chaos.
I gathered fragments he had scattered:
Job, Dante, Milton uttered.

I rocked no babies at the breast:
this child I had was child enough.
Like Mary I was chosen, blessed
to bear this spirit through his life.
"Jerusalem in every man"
this grain of sand in Albion.

My love walked in a wild domain
I followed him as best I could
beyond the boundaries of the brain
half credible, half understood.
We turned our trials into art
hammered the work upon the heart.

Vermeer

Each one concentrates.

This one is reading a letter,
its impact seeps through hand and arm
to eyes, unseeing, that take it in.

This one is making lace,
leans over to find the minuscule point
where the needle must finely touch.

This one is pouring milk,
controls the weight of the jar
lest the least drop spill.

This one weighs in the balance

as they all do,
even the astronomer who spins
the globe. If the balance is right
life goes on.
one fraction out and
we are destroyed.

Nature and Art

I. Kodo Drummer Interviewed

I run and wrestle.
You need to be strong to drum.
To drum you use your whole body
and control your breath.
You do not get carried away
by excitement and rhythm.
You are always in control.
Without control there is no passion.
It is not a religion—
drumming is an art.

II. Gravedigger Interviewed

I was still at school when I dug my first grave.
Someone has to do it.
Mechanical diggers? Over my dead body—
though my son would never let that happen.
 My graves are dug to measure for each coffin:
when it is dropped dead centre
you will find a three-inch margin
and depth five-foot-three:
less is disrespectful, more touches water.
Graves are exacting labour.
It is my work. I take pride in it.
It demands all my strength.

III. Film Maker Interviewed

When I've made a film I think "Never again,
never again will I go through that travail."
But then I fear I may not make another.
Did I find happiness? I never looked for it.
I don't know what you mean.
Sorrow is more important: sorrow
for the imperfection in all we try
to do, in each film, in each
demand of beauty and of truth.

IV. Mother Interviewed

It is my life. I delight in it.
You must control your breath.
It takes all your strength.
You use your whole body.
You think "Never again,
never again will I go through
such travail." But then you fear
you may not have another.
Happiness? There is none
to compare: happiness
for the perfection
that has come to pass.

2 Contemplative

Conception I

Copernicus imagined revolutionary orbs
and their celestial movement, uniformly
circular, the axiom of astronomy; and Shelley
saw Allegra stretch out her arms to him,
dead dream-child in the shore's wild foam
        where he would drown
        on 8th July, a chance storm—
Leonardo might have accurately
depicted the coil of each eddy—
        a whirlwind that would raise
        such fateful double-spiral force.

Conjunction that wrought wreck, death,
collusion or collision, like the typhus
fever that killed Allegra in Venice
left alone with nuns, her last breath—
born to appear this immortal wraith.
        Poems were also written,
        stories, epics, novels, Byron
and Claire, Jane and Shelley, Mary's babies
died and Keats had died and still they
        thought of better worlds, white radiance,
        jouissance, the planetary plan of justice.

Conjugation of verbs, to be, to bide, *ich bin,*
to make a bield on earth, to conjoin
forces for good, safety, communion.
I build therefore I am. The tide
cannot erase the words he made
        or the history they were composed of
        or our guilt that beauty, even truth,
should be destructive and chaotic.
Did order come with reason and scientific
        method, the Grand Orrery,
        logarithms, algebra and geometry?

Mars was Lord of the fifth house
and Jupiter in the ascendant;
Venus, rarely, in transit, Mercury present
across the face of the sun; clash
of humours merely, consciousness
                a word, say animal, say angel,
                    messenger, energy field, electrical
or resonant, in memoriam
nowhere, the message the medium,
                where atoms dance and stars emanate,
                    ideas encounter, encircle, magnificate.

Conception II

We shall conceive ourselves anew, transcend
a passive sense of being born or dying
as if we were inert—like stones or sand.

Mutability masked, these are defying
the drag of entropy and fragmentation
by sheer mass and number, like the flying

of knots in flocks to arctic destination
to nest alone and hatch a single chick
which joins again the polar transmigration.

Nothing is inert that has not thickened
from a pulse, a wilful, mental signal
of mere nerve, an unforensic flicker.

The sperm swarm surfs onward, ripples
conduct, call from the womb and one rides
into the eye of the ovum, its dark pupil,

as into a star's black hole it rushes to hide
in its own swelled head, merges naked of membrane
with the egg's cytoplasm as nuclei coincide,

as chromosomes combine and zygote, the one
essential factor for making a quite new thing,
is released for conception to begin.

What an idea, what preparation, to bring
such a host of particulars into order
and sustain the measure, the balance, matching

wholes that are halves to cross over the border
into a *déjà vu* yet uniquely novel whole,
as cells divide and genes draw up each feature.

Nativity, to come to be or begin, a free fall,
whatever we think—explode, escape, expand,
let chaos have its way and mind its will.

We conceive ourselves anew, reform, rebuild
a common weal, an open plan, a wisdom field.

Conception III

I am, not yet, a part of my mother, yet not...
apart from my father, yet he continues through me
or the chromosomes and genes that are growing me,
coded yet free, predestined yet coincidental.

I am— incarnate, très immature, washed ashore
from that internal sea: mare, maria, mother,
and forced to breathe, to fill my lungs with air,
the necessary pneuma if I am to find voice.

What I am—chatter-box, bundle of raw emotion,
given a name, called names, embraced,
abandoned, fed, starved, left in the dark,
brought to light, wrapped and unwrapped

like some strange gift to the world
and to someone's particular life, certain
circumstances, woven into a family,
a people, into this complex soul of things.

How was the moment chosen of conception?
What decided the instant of my birth?
Who winds the stars and sets the attractions
that plot our coagulation, our manifestation?

It is life the liver, whose tiny urges come
to the surface, gell, dwell, stick, stay,
gather moss for a while on a patch of earth:
I happened here, therefore—*ecco*—must be

Or become? There is no stopping still until
death, transubstantiation.
To walk upright is a ridiculous craze.
To let go, go on, onward, refuse to fall,

Consciously, warily, tread to the edge of each circle,
beyond, make what *I will* of myself, like the lark
ascending, I create and am caught in a company
of ideas, a communion to witness, *creando pensamus.*

I ought to be beautiful, good and true and
I can conceive, nativitate, live and grow,
transform by death, all in the active mode,
for *I am* a whole that makes holy an infinite.

Conception IV

As pilgrims sleep after each day's advance
we shelter as best we may where hostel or inn,
barnyard or wayside hut make room for us.
We sleep to rest.

We take no thought for the morrow except to keep
in the right direction and in good health and humour
with companions. We jest and talk
and fall silent

to succour each other in pain or injury, to calm
our terrors. We share any victuals and blankets
and aught we receive from alms.
We rest to sleep.

We keep no vigil awake in the dark, aching, sad,
in dread of daylight or fear of the haunting past.
We know we have come far and must go forward
day after day

in purpose, not waiting for what befalls.
We choose the route and distance. We appoint the shrine
and endow it with hopes. The sight of it will call forth
our unused powers.

*   *   *

We enter the tomb to stretch in the presence
of relics, the inmost circle. We fast and pray and then
lie down to sleep or watch on the sacred ground.
We sleep to dream.

Circumscribed yet open, separated yet with a gate
to go in and come out, the temple is kept pure
by our ritual, by water and the removal of shoes.
It is empty space.

This real world, yet apart, is asylum and yet
demands the sternest adherence to rules.
Here is the presence in which we present
our travelled flesh,

oursouls in *embonpoint* and fall down to sleep,
putting aside all else, make free our hands, minds,
to recover what we surrender or what we are given to know.
Our voice is thin.

As Samuel slept, a child, he heard his name. The temple dream
is granted to innocents who dare to wait in the precinct
and wake in the dark, without preconception
of who they are.

When we emerge we bear the stigmata deep in the psyche
and speak strange words in our awkwardness—as secret
new equations begin their working within our frame
towards consummation.

Maiden Aunts

Aunt Ella, Belle and Jane
> *three sisters bright and beautiful*

lived together or alone
for the men had mostly died
thousands killed, unmarried
in the first World War.
The girls they'd waited for
had no chance of a husband then
> *none for Ella, Belle or Jane.*

Ella became a headmistress
> *three sisters bright and beautiful*

an excellent teacher and linguist
with influence far and wide
over pupils, her joy and pride—
and for me, her only niece,
all sorts of unwanted advice:
I was sent away to school
> *because Ella's word was rule.*

Jane died early of cancer.
> *three sisters bright and beautiful*

Her energies turned against her
finding nowhere else to go
in their wit and fun and flow.
Practical, she raised poultry
and laughed and loved poetry.
Warm and kind and sane
> *was my excellent aunt Jane.*

What can I say about Belle
> *three sisters bright and beautiful*

the prettiest of them all?
Disappointment turned her mouth down.
She complained from dawn to sundown.
She lavished her affection
on dogs, her only children.
Born to be a perfect mother
> *Auntie Belle. It was denied her.*

Aunts Ella, Belle and Jane
three sisters bright and beautiful
I remember you all with pain
and wish you had each been given
the choice of motherhood. Even
adoption was disallowed
without a husband. You took no vow
of celibacy or religion.
Your fate was to be woman.

Ella, Jane and Belle
three sisters bright and beautiful
who lived decently and well.
But then I had no cousins.
Men laid down the conditions
about children, one or many,
and who could not have any.
It was wasteful, bleak and cruel
for Ella, Jane and Belle.

Jane, Belle and Ella
three sisters bright and beautiful
virginity a kind of hell,
despised, denied, rejected,
hypocritically respected.
Now we can turn this upside down,
make spinsterhood the highest crown:
let fertility now avail
for every Ella, Jane and Belle.

Tantus Labor Non Sit Casus
(Let such labour not be useless)

I stand as Mary below the cross: *stabat mater*.
I have seen the pure, sacred body of my loved-one
taken up on the nails, hung to prolong his pain.

I see the clarity of his temperament and every delicate feature,
the lines around eyes and mouth, the brow, the bones of his feet,
head and hands, the lean and kindly stretch of the arms,

the body I used to wrap in the silk of my embraces,
the head I used to take to my breast
and cradle on the curves of my womb

the one I held in familiar, daily caress
has been lashed on high and made to believe
there is freedom in such suspension.

Lords of the universe and queens of all that is green,
tender, innocent and loyal, gather your graces
and save this man, this one you created, vulnerable, perfect.

I name the relief worker, forced to watch
while a child died of starvation:
the eyes of the long-dead boy could never be extinguished.

I name Stella, who shone like her name with compassion,
who expended her life in rescuing refugees
ravaged and mutilated from Europe or Asia.

The temple of the body is to be revered,
for this is the substance we dwell in, our home,
our communal shelter in daily endeavour,

in fullness and in welcoming proud humility
as I opened to him the doors of my dwelling,
my lowly lintel, my own magnificat.

Let such labour not be useless, let
my fingers take up the pen and compose
the music of pain and lasting lament,

my outrage at this defilement, this scoring, scarring
of my beloved, his neck where I rested
my lips, my head, and stroked

his every part to touch, as if to restore
his childhood with gentle endearment,
the innocent godly shape that grew within him

and lives, despite the molestation of violent deaths
and of slow, unloving cruelties;
that grows and grafts a new and fragrant flowering

out of such loving, the labour the universe suffers
to bring forth, after aeons, exquisite persons
whose limbs, with each finest hair, are numbered and noted

and now have been crucified, have been torn
in their seamlessness, to be broken
and yet redeemed, reborn in each generation
by lingering, sorrowful, watching, maternal love.

The Unquiet Poem

The unquiet poem is patient.
It listens to arguments and
hears out discussions
but says nothing.

The unquiet poem does not
agree or disagree. It cannot
utter because it thinks
in different words.

The unquiet poem's lips
sometimes move. It almost
makes to speak. It feels
there is an answer ...

but to another question.
The poem is unquiet
waiting for the right
form of question.

The unquiet poem is contained
as tides swell the harbour
but floating under water
are wrecks of living things

dropped down by commerce
from the trading world.
The voice of the poem
is also assumed drowned.

The unquiet poem wants
to crawl from sea to land.
It attends a signal
whether dark or light.

That sound is not quiet
even when softly spoken.
It releases valves of speech,
the violent word: love.

Icy Swimmers

A heron has stalked here over the snow
unerringly to the river and lonely
as ever positions himself by a stump
humped as he waits.
                    I follow the tracks
and watch as he stretches his neck
higher, holds it, until my presence
is as tree or bush, while water
laps the melting bank with fish:
icy swimmers.
                   Working indoors
I know the heron wades there, alone
day and night, crumpled by wind
or stiffened by frost, stands
awaiting his chance. His life
depends on it—even as mine
has come to depend on the chance
of steadfastness such as his.

At School

As in a film I see brown lace-up shoes
and brown lisle stockings
held by suspenders that dragged
dragged us down—
shoes that plied through dark brown leaves
along St Andrews' *Scores*
and up steps across the paving into
that cold brown house where I was kept
as if a prisoner, one of fifty.

At basement level like a moat around
the house were railings and spikes and
everywhere stone walls, my desolation.

Birds may have sung and trees flowered,
grass may have grown and weeds bloomed,
but we lived darkly in brown:
thick brown tunic, thin brown cardigan,
brown felt hat, coat and gloves,
brown paint on doors and skirtings,
furniture brown and brown linoleum.

No music except hymns,
no poetry save the Bible,
no talking, no running,
no nonny no sense.

In dull fear, sometimes acute,
we lived in solemn loneliness
yet in a crowd, like prisoners
waiting, waiting for release.

When at last it came
we were no longer children.

Russian Doll

Like a Russian doll I know my body
is encompassed by layers of spirit force
where the gashes it has suffered
are sealed and knit again
and all my flesh is held pristine and clear.

This undying body is the inmost and the utmost.
I make a vow: no more needles, probes or tests.
What you see is the time-bound manifestation
of the shape my courage takes.

It has chosen weaker stuff
where the weave is looser and
light shines through.
I unpick heavy bindings,
chain stitches, linings
and the double hems.

Is it a sampler? This spells my name,
my age, identity. I read the
neat hatchings of my child fingers.
It sews my maiden name, outlines
my spirit cover, my Russian-doll design.

This is my Body

Cut to the heart I hear
the woman behind the curtain beside me:
"Thank you doctor, thank you.
You are most kind I know
you saved my life by cutting off my breast.
Excise now what you think best:
my ovaries, the left breast?"

In our humiliation and mutilation
we do not question that he has
our individual good at heart,
rather than his research, beneath
his wholesome white-coated front.

He parts my curtains. I refuse all
to be on the safe side-further operations.
Amazed he shrugs: "It's your body."
I know it is. I choose to choose my treatment.
He warns I will regret it. *So he knows
what's best but still continues the research.*

I stick to my guns—a phrase by which he means
I do not go along with his proposals.
I vow no more drugs. No more needles
probed in my already-gashed breast.
In tears of doubt I am dismissed.

Honey
for my mother

I hate to see you eating sliced bread
and pasty honey you have to smear
from a plastic crucible, tearing back
the thin cover with inaccurate fingers

when honey used to ooze for you from the comb
to spread and share without stint, the
very bees flew for you and flowers opened
in the Spring of your country childhood

that you cannot recover as in your dreams.
Yet I see it today with your memory's eye
and you as Titania, uncrowned, but queen
of the cowslip field and the bluebell wood.

.

The Night-Walking

Why does she walk about in the night,
climb out of bed and over the edge
of rail or bar, to stumble
and search and wake the sleeping?

What does her wandered mind desire
in the night that cannot be found again
and is laid to rest by day
in the stir of faces and voices?

Who does she think she is as she gropes,
falls out of bed and breaks her bones
in crying need to get out
of this place, this prison of flesh?

Where does she want to go in the night,
in the corridor, tunnel that has no end
or leads to a sleep she cannot
allow herself to succumb to?

When will it cease, this walking to nowhere?
Are her babies lost? Has her mother left her?
Brothers and sisters have gone
and the husband, depended on.

Her daylight is done. Her dark is ever.
Those she belongs with are calling her, hauling her.
Do not resist any longer:
sleep my darling, my mother.

The Cry

I know it's not a cry of pain
ah lack-a-day I say
(the sound goes to the brain)
more, recognition of a state
of loss or lurking sense of fate
in childhood's long delay.

The cry is one of being apart
ah lack-a-day I say
(the sound goes to the heart)
it is himself who's absent
soon he'll run into the present
and take his time to play.

The cry is one in which we share
ah lack-a-day I say
(the sound is hard to bear)
our overlapping lives belong
a half-remembered catch of song
for ever and today.

I hear him crying when I phone
ah lack-a-day I say
(the sound goes to the bone)
his Dad says he's fed up with him
his Mum is doing other things
and I am far away.

"The soul is not in the body but the body is in the soul" (Meister Eckhart)

Leonardo bought caged birds to set them free.
A little boy I know gets his mother
to buy a plant whenever they shop
at Tescos *to rescue them.*
Does he sense their helplessness
from his?
          How can I reassure him
he is no caged bird, no uprooted fern?

His soul bears him everywhere;
it shines into his body
and wings and sings about him
to draw out his hidden
coiled leaves and stored
rapture of flowers.

Folded to be free he is bought
at great price: our dreams,
our love for him.

Trains Pass my Window

Trains pass by day
packaged with people.
They attend the signal
to enter a destination
the same for all:
tourist, pilgrim, messenger.

Trains glide in darkness
empty as they go but
muttering with blue
underworldly light on
row on row of seats
where no one sits.

In the lively mid of night
dim human figures tap
and mend the rails,
the sleepers, by lantern flare
before some engine brings
its rolling cargo through.

Such passing emotions:
new-car carriers
overloaded intercities
quiet empty coaches
and trucks filled with "goods."

They come and go and carry
urgent travelling feelings,
mere passengers or whims.
I do not always look out
or go to the window.
I can tell by listening
which I should ignore.

By Night

Night after night I drove
A hundred miles or more of twisting track
I travelled to my love
I carried heavy grief
It thickened in my heart and broke my back.

He lay in hospital
With drip and monitor and mask and wires
He could not move at all
Death waited for his call
While fever seared his veins   his lips   with fires.

Each night I held his hand
He faintly strove to live   to breathe   to speak
I tended him   I smiled
He cried   he was a child
A dynasty of strength now made him weak.

Then after many days
He uttered   craved some honey on the tongue
I knew this was a sign
The one essential thing
If life could yet be heroically won.

Among the expert teams
Of scientific staff and equipment
No drop of honey gleams
No dew   no clear streams
From Nature for the human predicament.

I knew it fell to me
To set out on this mission   his request
Late night I drove the car
I found the honey jar
But sore by then in desperate need of rest.

I asked for help in vain
None understood that gods were in command
I set out then again
At midnight and in pain
And stumbled with the honey to the ward.

My love now lives anew
And day by day regains a little power
As wise as it is true
The things we have to do
Are for each other any time or hour.

The Passenger

I came to the banks of the Lethe
and approached the ferryman:
I asked how much he charged
for a single, no return.

I looked across the river
as it rippled in the breeze
then stepped into the rowing-boat
as he took up the oars.

Your fare, he said, for crossing
in this weather, on this night
is your last drawn breath
and your last eye-light.

Will you take a poem instead:
I have one in my throat?
But it swelled there choking
with wads of paper notes.

My blood it is the stream
my breath it is the wind
my body forms the boat
for the ferryman: my mind.

Two Halves

My face is a-symmetric
    the right side full and smiling
    the other fierce, determined.

The halves would fuse together
    but now it seems as if
    they accentuate their difference.

Even in my eyes
    the colours are distinct:
    one brown, the other greener.

* * * * * *

I overheard them talking:
    I must get this work done
    and done as best I can.

And the right side was teasing:
    It will cost you your living
    your friends and your beloveds.

The other only asked:
    And what am I to them
    If I have no dedication?

To which came the reply:
    The world needs its workers
    but forgets to reward them.

Reward? scoffed the left,
    Do you think I think like that?
    The work gives its consolation.

What's the matter then?
    was the nonchalant rejoinder,
    Some like to work, some play,

* * * * * *

And some play at work
    while for others work is play—

As my two half faces say.

Counting

Those who count
                can count
and those who don't count
                don't

Now the counters want to invent
a way of counting what can't be counted

The counters need counters
to account for the unaccountable

It gets them back to square one

Meanwhile those who don't count
don't count on it

They count themselves lucky

There's nothing to it really

3 Discursive

In Praise of Libraries

One

Here you will find words strangely
Strung together, made into poems and

Somewhere the one that is designed for you.
A soldier found the anthology

He had to jettison from his kit
On campaign in the Caucusus in 1941.

An engineer found "The Sleeping Lord"
As David Jones traced his contours:

The latent dragon energy
Of our floating island earth.

We know the causes of death,
We study and research them.

Of life we know nothing and
Great libraries have been burnt

And aeons of accumulated vital
Knowledge has been destroyed.

We recollect fragments in poems, songs,
Paintings, to restore the pattern.

Here is a country for the brave to explore.
Here be dragons: in this tiny library.

Two

In the street of Canopus east to west
where the Dogons walked, their heads in the stars,
from Gate of the Sun to Gate of the Moon
the world's wisdom was scrolled and shelved.

Within Museum and Serapeum,
a succession of scholars and translators,
a clutch of rulers who wanted the power
of knowledge as well as gold and battle.

Lost in fire, destroyed by burning,
mobbed by murderers, neglected, buried,
sold abroad, copied and travestied,
collected privately, scattered again—

A place *for the Cure of the Soul* in Thebes,
a place for the Law of the Jews in Egypt,
a place for algebra in Asia,
a place for the music of Greece in Rome.

Christians thought they knew the answers,
erased all temples and sacred writings.
The whim of priest or wish of Caliph
replaced mathematics and scholarship.

By bread alone we have never lived
but fed by parchment, scroll and vellum
among the fusty-heads who guard them:
chant Alexandria, Pergamum.

In the street of Canopus east and west
we'll walk like Dogons, heads in the stars,
from Gate of the Sun to Gate of the Moon
while secret wisdom-crystals shine.

One speck may lie in a book of poems,
one beam be found in a book of dreams,
physics or anthropology. The bookshelf
of history winds and waits for

Souls to catch up. See them winged,
watch them change from lead to gold.
The hidden shall be found again,
the speed of light shall be excelled.

Three

Sceptical Neleus, son of Coriscus, friend
of Aristotle, returned to Troas bearing
books: the works of the master, bequeathed to him.

Strato was appointed to the School in Athens
with paraphrases and general principles,
no chain of logic, no unravelled sleeve
of careful reasoning. These belonged to Neleus
whose descendants buried them in the ground.

Ptolemy Philadelphus purchased what he believed were
"Aristotle's books". So they were. The very books
Aristotle had owned. Not the ones he had written.

Romans came searching for them. Dug up and sold,
damp and damaged, exposed to wars and dogma,
they passed from hand to careless hand and disappeared.

Four

The palace of Alexandria,
shaped like a *chlamys*, a widespread cloak,
opened its domains for the feast of Adonis.
Women lamented the lovely youth
"our hair unbound,
our garments untied,
our breasts uncovered,"
they carried him to the shore.

And returning to the palace
the people were restored
in gymnasia, theatre,
odeon for music therapy,
platform for dreaming: all
that saves us from slavery to
the opposing emotions of pity and fear—
and books, a feast of them
sheaths unbound, ribbons untied
and truth itself uncovered.

Five

Of what use are books without number,
complete collections, catalogues,
if the owner has no time even to read
the titles? Seneca's question and answer:
"Not for study but for display."

Better a few books loved and known
than volumes unopened. Or better
one sacred book and nought that contradicts?
Amr, general to Omar
despatched the Museum's books
for fuel to the public baths.
It took six months to burn them.

Thus did the thoughts of the ancients
wash over the bodies of mercenaries
and thus did the Saracens
enjoy the fruits of their victory.

Six

Scrolls: hidden
in perfume jars within mountain caves.
Not worth stealing for thousands of years,
not gold or silver but crumbling parchment.
The past is not priceless until the present
is worthless.

A goat-boy fell upon them by chance
and scholars of all the world
prey delicately upon them, while
wars and fires and missiles and massacres
continue as before
and *The Teacher of Righteousness*
passes through the midst of us.

Seven

In convents and crypts, in kists and coffins,
tiny illuminations;
in private collections chained and padlocked
or dusty, oak-panelled institutions
where sunlight canticles on a spine,
a gold-leafed title: *The Golden Bough;*
or moonlight charms the pallor of
a forgotten *Woman in White;*
or a girl from the country slits apart
a thick, warm page of cavorting Sanscrit;
or on paper as thin as a butterfly wing
holds a pocketbook of proverbs.

Books, too precious to keep,
too tough to destroy, too
dangerous to trust, too
charged with truth, too
silent in face of violence, too
volatile for the screen, books
are thoughts in transit, they gather
as they go more and more rolling beauty.
Who knows who shall know?
Whom will the finger touch?

Scottish Education

Dipped in the river of learning—*curriculum*
banked and channelled in narrow courses,
The Scottish Child is held by its Alma Mater
but, like Achilles, one heel remains
unsteeped, pointedly Scottish, dry, disbelieving.

From this unindoctrinated heel, this
tenderfoot, this easily wounded patch
we have to form again the entire
body of Scottish Studies, trace its outline
and recreate the flesh of our living future.

River

Light flows with the river:
broadly calmly the force
of all those deeps is contained
although each winter turf by turf
the banks give way and fall.

Birds fly with the river:
loudly lowly the speed
of all those wings is directed
and each Spring in reed and sand
they build anew their nests.

Trees grow with the river:
blown and bent the persistence
of all those leaves bears fruit
and branch and flower festoon their own
reflection in the pools.

Feelings flow, ideas fly and
peace grows with the river:
we nest our hearts
and trail our leaves
in that deep reflection
as the river takes it.

Kingfisher

Kingfisher blue
bluer than sky
skyer than air
more air than water
more water than leaf
more leaf than light
lighter than stream
more stream than ray
more ray than russet
more russet than daybreak

blue   sky   air
water   leaf   light
stream   ray   russet
daybreak   blue

I saw you not once
not twice but three times

What is your message
bluebird, tell me?

I wait I tremble
it will come   it will come
out of the blue

Light and Soul

Freddy Hudson, you were fun
incarnate in a big man
with bald head and one arm.

To amuse us kids you
lit your cigarette
using only the stump.

Although they said you'd
"lost your arm in Burma"
I was only seven or eight
and did not imagine the wounding:
knives, grenades, searing pain.

But today, when I watched
the Chindits at "White City"
and with their mules on
monsoon jungle tracks—
some "road to Mandalay"—

Suddenly you were present
Freddie Hudson, winking,
joking beside me
as you lit that cigarette.

To Norman MacCaig for his Birthday 1995

I know you do not like my poems much
and have already books enough and more,
so this is just a way of being in touch.

I've given you my books of poems, which
you've mostly managed quietly to ignore:
I know you do not like my poems much.

Untalented, unbeautiful, unrich
I am, and all agree *how great you are!*
This is my modest way of being in touch.

I cannot cook and have no other such-
like useful skills you might adore,
and I know you do not like my poems much...

Yet they are me and cannot be detached
from what I think and feel for you, Norman.
This is my loving way of being in touch.

Roundabout Tree

I climbed a high crag
one ice-bright, sun-cut morning
and scanned the makars' city
below me, faintly roaring.

Cars crawled like insects
leaving poison trails.
They scuttled through the arteries,
clogged the city squares.

I saw a clump of trees
newly planted, slender-stemmed,
dizzy on a roundabout
where traffic geared and jammed.

I descended the steep cliff
to interview a sapling;
could hardly cross the road
for vehicles encircling.

At last I made a dash—and
reached the waiflike tree.
This island was her home.
She was imprisoned publicly.

Unaware of any other
kind of lifestyle, the young tree
grew bravely as she would
in the wild country.

But as she grew taller
she could see on the skyline
oaks and beeches swaying,
clouds and birds flying.

Poor tree had no escape from
din and dirt, fumes and fear.
She questioned her relations:
"Why have we been planted here?"

"We suffer to save the world,"
they told her. "By our leaves
we balance heat and water,
make it easier to breathe.

Blackbird and starling
rest on our topmost branches
and their song can be heard
in the loudest city noises."

The young tree was not sure
if she cared to be a martyr.
She'd much prefer to grow
in a meadow by the river.

I pitied the helpless youngster
with no chance of change, no hope,
condemned to this pollution,
never to reach full growth.

I turned to climb again
up the crag to blue freedom,
crossed the road, left the tree
to its tragic situation.

* * *

I stopped by two months later
sheltering from April showers,
looked up and saw a dazzling
canopy... of flowers.

The Poet as Woman

Poets as women are self-destructive
like Plath, who felt flayed alive,
or Sappho, her poetry valued only for
the womanhood, the pretty face or
silly passion, deviance or distress
its maker can profess.
                        Germaine
falls over backwards to maintain
women both think and feel
in treatises
on how our bodies suffer,
especially if we do *not* offer
them severed from our heads
but take our books to bed.

The poet as woman must write trustingly,
aroused mentally and lustingly.
She creates her children, her satisfaction
word by word, her own conception:
the lineaments of gratified desire—
mind that joy: it is a tree on fire.

Tradition

I wish I were
a medieval
melancholy madonna,
eyebrows lifted in a strange surprise,
looks downcast in vague delight
at my cuddly manchild.

I wish I were encircled
by a decorative lily
protective rosa munda,
veiled and loosely covered
in wide empyrean garments,
tiny gold incisions
in my traditional halo.

Three Trees

Three trees grow in the wilderness,
sturdy, straight and high,
apart and far from Paradise
with roots and spreading branches,
that meet in the starspun sky.

The first is the tree of Goodness,
thick and gnarled as the oak:
a way for those who will sacrifice
pleasure for duty, pay the price
and live by the rule and the book.

The second is the tree of Truth,
smooth and clean as the beech:
a way for those who will seek and test,
and travel in perpetual quest
to the bourne we seldom reach.

The third is the tree of Beauty,
supple with grace as the ash:
a way for those who must create
a moving thought, a dynamic state,
the form of the wings of the wish.

To climb the height of any of these
is to find where the treetops meet,
a wholiness shed over generous earth
to encompass death and suffer birth,
where each is in all complete.

Rondel for the Yew

The yew stands darkly by the door,
      Which is older, house or tree?
      Which keeps the other company?

The yew is green throughout the year,
Dances with the wind and weather
      Like the Queen of Faerie.
The yew stands darkly by the door,
      Which is older, house or tree?

Those bowing arms were used for war
      To quicken arrows on their way.
      We strangely bow our heads today:
Life and death those branches bear,
      The yew stands darkly at the door.

Relatively Speaking

Between music and mathematics lies the comma.
Between Pythagoras and Orpheus find the point
of no return. Once crossed the pass lies
only onward to another range of equilibrium.

Play a chord and try to sing it.
You cannot. The intervals are spaced
to correspond with harmonies of tone in colour
and with rhythmic growth in plants.

By the ratio of planets to our sun,
their elliptic paths and predestined cycles
we are kept in time and season
with a precision equally applied to each
earthly creature here or deep below the sea.
A slight oscillation can destroy.

The precession of the equinoxes may have
moved a continent beneath the polar ice.
When Sirius was close to earth he rose
brighter than the moon, and still
beneath the sphinx in *son et lumière*
the desert dogs will howl.

The balance that conditions livingness
to be and to become, to be sustained,
is bound to justice, hard to estimate.
No line is marked. We have to devise it
with care, taking care, burdened with it
but at the same time leaving all to chance.

We try to manage the coincidence or
plot the births and deaths, arrange
the marriages. The counterpoint to Science
is hidden yet revealed to sense
when sense itself is in suspense.

* * *

Music is our wisdom and our word promises.
Memory is luminiferous, a trail
of particles, electric whorl, wave-field
that passes through obstructions and reforms,
an almost logical equity within totemic circles.

Balance, place, diversity, relations,
our honky tonk, our plangeancy
our plodding on to life beyond
each death, our alternating radiances.

Waiting

The image is of stillness, intransitive,
and yet it takes a mountain's mass
of energy to wait, with objective
or without, whether we guess
what is to come or, futureless
we're vigilant, instinctive.

We wait perpetually for future grief
yet occupy ourselves, to leave no space
for it. With it comes relief
from cramped dread; then the press
of pain, like the tide, races
in its own time against our barrier reef.

I accommodate departure and return,
make room for one to die. It is expected.
But with the loss a pattern
of attention will be changed, directed
now towards the unforeseen, an awaited
stillness in the sea, movement in mountain.

Vox Humana

He sings like a bird from
the diaphragm, the whole
body, the chest that gives
volume equal to many birds:
four and twenty blackbirds
they all began to sing.

The sound is huge from a child:
his three-year-old frame
transforms to an instrument
for deep howls of music, for
wails and long sustained
notes of sheer human-being.

He starts from what he feels
he knows: exults like
the dog in chase, his bike
look how fast,
the low-flying jet
or the taste of goats' ice-cream.

Sing, sing, Oscar Samuel!
You hear the human sound
of wordless ancestors, of the
earth you tread, its shining beetles,
of the sky you breathe, the buzzard,
of shells, pebbles, water.

He sees, touches, tastes, lets
music break the bounds of
his body, sets sound free,
escapes barriers of pain
and limits of dependence
to become more what he is:

A huge rebel spirit charged with
angelic powers, a growing creature:
cells, limbs, thoughts, eyelashes,
new and unique in the universe,
a beauty beyond words yet
pas idéal as he tends to say of things.

Le Grand Collier Argenté

"Here the day begins empty," she told me,
"and then fills up. You do not plan.
You go with the flow." It sounded like
the practice of negative capability.
I could see what she meant and how
when two or three were met, others
would adhere and a party was let loose:
"très cool," says my little Mowgli.

The day began full for me with open promise
of sunrise through the window that looked
upon *la Place*, whose three linden trees
were pricking with green buds beside
a high wrought-iron cross; its halo
beamed with light from the wide mountain.

Bees abounded in white peach blossom
by the bench where I was reading.
"They are making honey." A bird-in-song
is framed in a blue zig-zag of sky.
Mowgli now is playing with his friends
on their bikes. They jump off and run
to pee against the tree.

Mowgli is stalking an orange papillon:
gold-flame with a border of black pearls:
le grand collier argenté says the book.
It flits among dandelions, a tawny sunbeam.
"The caterpillar sleeps in moss and wakes
a butterfly"—after feasting on violets.

Violet is thus transformed to Gold.
"You can eat *les pensées* too,"
says Mowgli and crushes some on his tongue.
They grow like weeds, passionately;
the dog watches patient but alert;
we hang the washing out above the world.
I love this little boy, this empty day.

Note: les pensées = pansies/violets, and thoughts

In Keeping

1

John Berger's *Pages of the Wound,*
poems as "pages laid out to dry,"
I found in damp, jostly Cambridge
in freezing fog and Christmas lights
with Bach's *Magnificat* on CD
bought in the same shop-—
"et exsultavit spiritus meus."

2

Faded simplicity up and down
wooden stairs at Kettles Yard:
here the most modern artists of our century
wrestle to grow old gracefully
among pebbles, worn rugs and Japanese
visitors instructed by eager,
well-mannered, scholarly ladies.

3

Do not lean bicycles against this wall.
Students rely on bikes and bikes rely on walls
but the medieval fabric of our learning
is too fragile to sustain the steel handlebars
of crowded, pressing, eager youth.
We glimpse them through a lighted window
all looking in one direction, a lecture in progress?
Where is the inspiring don? A television set.
To *New Horizons?* No, only the goalposts.

4

We return to our raucous river Leithen
and our dignified river Tweed. Here we live
in Scotland and in keeping with the faith
we keep with poetry by keeping it
in old-fashioned print by modern means
and ourselves in touch though wounded,
relying on each other nor lacking exaltation
as we turn pages backwards both and
forwards at *le fin de siècle.*

4 Interpretive

Elegy in Autumn

Rain like rays lit by pale sun
at evening by Loch Ness beneath the cedar tree
beside the Abbey fort once built by Wade
to quell the clans—
                           Rain so fine
you see it only in this haze of light
that shimmers over deep water where
motor launches circle at the base
of ruined Castle Urquhart, its towers
and rowanberries, drops of blood,
blood upon the *sgian* before it's put to rest—

Rain so delicate we feel it on our faces
like the brush of tears and let it rest
there for sorrow of the story, for rue
of it, for songs and valour, for
pipes and ardour, for centuries endured
of callous cruelty, for every casualty,
for dull poverty amid outrageous beauty—

Rain so soft it clings like memory
of those who had to sail, starving
and dispossessed, away, the sons we long for
and girls who wove the patterns of our work
in the colours of our speech, gone, gone—

Rain so cold it trickles in our blood
and turns our humour to a wheeze or moan,
to leave us dour and laughterless: leaves
lost, loosed, withered, sun-struck, windswept—

Rain that slants like Autumn in us now.

Water and Fire

Leaves arranged on iron tables painted
white and on chairs. Yellow leaves and
they lie still and all around each
separately rests as it has delicately
fallen—

Now, unstirred, they decorate curvaceous
ironwork where no-one sits and no-one
"takes the waters." I am passing by
this afternoon as others did before:
those who

came in hope of remedy *to renew
the vital fire by their adventitious
heat and congenial principles.*
Rich and fashionable they travelled
to malinger.

In carriages and trains they came
to stroll, stiff with rheumatism,
among the yews, to sip at tables
and admire the view: the confluence
of Leithen and of Tweed.

*Most excellent against all diseases
proceeding of moist cause: forgetfulness,
shakings and lethargies,* this *chaos
of salts and mineral effluvia* enters
and conflows within my veins.

I leave the sycamore upon the white.
I leave the pleasant terrace in its
neglectedness. I smile a little drily
as I walk away downhill and summon all
my vital fires.

Island Compass

The cuckoo keeps calling above a copse
of close-clustered trees.
A pet lamb leaps beside the gate
a pet boat lies beside the loch
a pet car rusts at the kitchen door.

We face The North: mountains and hoary rock,
a circle of islands, secretive sea;
a moor of peat, the road—a causeway—
fends off lochans and broken shielings.

Here the track crosses the river
a pool where spawning salmon lay:
On the trek home from school one was lifted,
returned again to complete life's arc.

We reach a jetty where no boat waits
and find the croft whose family is lost.

But where is *mo ghràdh** and the many-blessed children;
brothers, cousins, friends, sisters,
who ran up the hill, dived off the rocks,
fished, played on the dun by the steading,
up the road to school again
and again to church?

Some died young, some in the war,
others went to a far country.
Three fell ill and died last year.
One has returned and stands alone—
alone in the graveyard beside the sea.

*   *   *

We face The West: wind-worn rock,
waves wild crashing in cliffs of spray
yet a sheltered machair where tiny violets
and vetches lead to a sand-blanched cove.
A golden plover and larks take wing.
We pick out pebbles of pure rock crystal
warm pink felspar, mica stars.
Sapphires are somewhere and copper ores.

*mo ghràdh = my loved-one

But where is the pony, the lean black cow,
long kitchen bench in the house at the end,
the last before the edge of the world?
Where are the folk who toiled to make
and build fields?

                    His collie at heel
an old man bends by a wheelbarrow.
He remembers crops of oats and barley.
Now nothing grows but the overgrown,
but stony ground and a drift of sheep.

*   *   *

We face The East: the town is fussy
with offices, agencies, galleries, guesthouses.
The ferry blows and a submarine is surfaced at bay.
Ancient peoples are on exhibition
in surmised versions of stones and temples.

The old school sprawls into concrete extensions.
The castle is empty, its walls graffiti,
its grounds littered. Only a golfcourse
keeps up appearances. The library is cramped
in portacabins. Shop-window-corners
show Bibles and hats with satin and feathers.

But where is the fishing fleet, loyal sailors
and shops with tackle, ropes and hawsers?
Where are the children who went to war?
Their names are harboured in every family.

*   *   *

We face The South and over the hills
towards long beaches in low gold sun.
Turquoise water turns on the tide and deeper blues
reflect the clouds. Nothing but birds and shells
are gleaming, or is that a yacht coming
round the point? Another long loop and
a chain of isles for seal and otter and
boats at moorings and shadow and seaweed
and dying light.

The cuckoo keeps calling beside the church
that is only used as a shelter for tombs;
round the ruined Temple of Holy Blood
it flies and falls, echoes and fades.

The barren schoolhouse and walled playground,
forgotten villages, daisy-fields,
a circle of islands, of generations.

Where is the centre and where the edge
when are we leaving and when returning?

The Bones of Columba
The Brecbennach

for the new Museum of Scotland

We carry within us the bones of Columba
that carried him into adventure
through the dark age he illumined.

Wise in law, rash in prayer,
peregrinator and protector:
island to island the currents run.

He ploughs our waves of power and war
and harvests scattered tribes of longing
with runes to read, communion bread.

Bones of blessing, *brecbennach,*
at Monymusk in jewelled casket,
in principle justly among us.

Croft

The grazing place of cattle
         on the rounded seaward slope
The passing through, gateway
         between rocky outcrops

The brow of the hill, *suncatcher,*
         and marshy burn below
Make feeding grounds for sheep

The place for corn to grow is
         in *the minstrels' gallery*
where lark and curlew call

The fallow-field with hens and pony
         waits for seed to fall

These pieces form my land
         parts that I make fit together
strength of hoe, scythe and spade
         bank of peat against the winter

Children gather dulse and shells
and swim around *the place of seals*

Love of folk, place, work
names that make light in the dark.

The Clearances Recollected

We were given a tea-kettle, tub or blankets,
took turns to carry our brothers and sisters.
Arms, shoulders, backs were laden; creels
held babies, or even old folk, crippled.

Cattle we had to abandon, and even the dogs.

Shaking with anger we hurried to pack:
everything neat, nicely tied and thorough.

The bailiffs came and roughly herded us,
dragged the old ones out and left them on the hill.
Then they set the thatch alight: only
smoke coiled up in bitter revolt.

We walked, dazed, trailed the ones in front,
not knowing where we were going or why
we had to leave. We remembered precious things
we had not taken, the peats we'd cut
and thick milk in basins set for cream and cheese.

I stopped with my aching load and looked back
and I saw the factor throw
our milk upon the flames.

Lass o' Pairts

She read while crossing the road
she crossed the road while reading
a girl in Galashiels
      read a book
and walked across the busy main street
on Saturday when the signal gave her
green for go—go across—go on—
go on reading—absorbed in her book
absorbed by the traffic and clatter
she continued, streetwised, nine or ten,
a shelpit lass, a bookish lass, *puella docta*.

At a pedestrian-crossing we usually
hurry across, apologetic at holding
back the seas of traffic—for a person.
We hardly believe it can stop for
the fragile on foot. We look both ways
to be sure, are comforted by the bleeps.
As soon as we're halfway over we know
the flow will merge behind
our red-sea miracle passage.

This child I've seen had faith
greater than Moses I'd say:
no rod, no Jehovah, just her book
(god knows what book), to divide
the waves as she heads for a land
of promise.

Ethiopia

Boyish priests in jewelled and tasselled headwear
Gold, embroidered robes on your puny shoulders
Simple, spiky crosses on high before you
Plaintif to Heaven.

Dark your faces, dark your embattled temples
Strutting tall, but tiny below the mountains
Crimson capes may cover a ragged garment
Shawls wrap your prayers.

Sacred shrine, Ark of the Covenant long
Hidden, rescued, hallowed by chanting hermit
Holy Grail of legend destroying those un-
Worthy to touch it.

Staff and incense; pilgrims in calm procession
Walk the mud-baked ground with umbrella open
Shade from drought that eats up the flesh while living
Flesh of the harvest.

Haile Selassie's lions did not roar more fiercely
Hunger roars like Satan in search of victims
Dust has dulled the topaz of Ethiopia
Carpets and music.

Stretched outside a carcase, a human being
Slowly dies, his limbs like the staff he carried
Children watch a future of death, finding
Naught for their comfort.

Where does wisdom dwell but beside the river?
Gihon flowed from Eden in ancient story
Compassed Ethiopia entirely, richly
Watered the country.

Thousand thousand strong was the host of *Zerah*
Thousand thousand weak is the host of famished
Refugees from homes, from their herds and holdings
Lowland or mountain.

Where is wisdom found in religious fighting?
Can the Ethiopian now change his skin? Or
Rather western races now change their frightened
Piling of weapons?

Nuclear weapons, missiles and submarines and
Chemicals and germs and investment specially
Given to such research. Where is wisdom hidden
Under such terror?

Testings, threats and boasting of winning. People
Die and land is desert and earth is poisoned
Sun and moon and planets themselves revolving
All to no purpose?

Priests and Coptic saints in your threadbare dresses
Chant your way with dignity, wear your beauty
Bear your crosses, walk with them one more season
Keep your own customs.

Wisdom's price is far above gold or topaz
Wisdom can flood suddenly like a river
Crosses raise the question of life, and place the
Death on our shoulders.

Praise Poem for the Borders

Air could not chance so keen so fine
on Spartan hills or on the heights
of Macchu Picchu or in Kashmir at the gate
of Paradise as here today on Lee Pen,
when last snow and first lambs
bloom in the sun
and the Leithen, marker of life,
throws off winter icicles
clinging to rock and twig
and laps up light with little tongues
let loose on this March morning
as if sprung forth on pilgrimage.

Turnips bestrew the muddy fields
and sleek crows dance attendance.
Lambs that were born in yesterday's blizzard
are dressed in plastic coats
and hop about to throw then off
like chicks from a broken shell.

No need to travel to Greece or Spain.
We are not led astray by Tourism.
Where would we see a flock of oyster-catchers
as they wheel over the water-meadows, and
the chaffinch in his new pink waistcoat,
ducks dabbling for nests
and the hawk alight on his post?

Where would we cross a pathway
striped with shadows of silver birch
or a bridge three hundred years old
over the river of battles, the Tweed,
flowing sedately, among its keeps
and castles, hydros and farmyards?

Where would ponies crop daffodils
up the hill and rub their matted coats
on a solitary pair of ancient oaks?

This air this land this March marvel
this fin de siècle this newborn joy
this moment unmemorable commonplace
repeated year after year without
warning—as the white hare
rises in snow and lopes off onto the moor
and his summer lifestyle—

This is more than cars or cruises
to me, more than flights:
this is what I love.

Cry for Help

Kipling wrote HELP ME in the basement
of the grim Holloways in Southsea
where he was boarded aged five from India
by his loving, artistic, educated parents,
for his own good.

No help came except from books.

He learnt to read and then all his life
he wrote. His heroes were resourceful
under all circumstances. Aesthetically
we create our own order, our own world
and we control it and so escape
our helplessness.

I like to try to put things in
order for aesthetic reasons.
Chaos and destruction upset me,
yet reality is chaotic.
Do we let it rip or cultivate
our garden or try to find the
patterns in it?

Saviours are born sometimes and
we follow them. The writing on the wall
cannot be ignored. It shouts our
desperation. We have taken action
and let go, now and again,
then and later, before and after.

"Poetry helps" is now admitted.
What a novel discovery! We create
our own attempt at order, rhythm,
meaning. Good. It is good.
I'm writing on the wall.
I seek a pattern in chaos:
HELP.

The Book Rediscovered in the Future

One day in the future
a child may come across a book
and say: "Imagine being able to hold
in your hand what you read,
to carry it with you and wear it out
with your life; to pass it on
bearing your marks, your name,
written in ink, your signature:
your wave-length in letters."

Chaos Rules

Behind the scenes, chaos;
on stage, order.
Does order create chaos
or chaos create order?

What appears chaos is composed
of multiple mini-order.
Each child controls her own corner:
costumes folded just so
for quick hands-on, quick changes;
shoes, make-up and floor space
possessed: en masse, yet
each one autonomous.

They have come from homes
all over the city with
plaited hair, practised feet:
one day, one week, that food,
some sleep, transport
planned around them.

The random world, the chaos
we feel so threatened by
is order in *minute particulars.*
More arbitrary is
the order we impose.

To create our own lives
or any peculiar thing
is to tune in and practise
until, like these dancers,
we are precisely in step
with each other and the music.

This will happen rarely.
Most of the time, daily,
we work behind the scenes
at the part that's ours to play.

To an audience it looks easy
yet the inside story tells,
glimpsed now and then,
chaos is the order of the day.

5 Relative

A Poem for Jean

"How can I enjoy it,"
she said, "unless I know
 it's good, until I prove it,
unless I undergo
the opposites that fuse it,
blow by counter-blow?"

When it works it feels like play
dances like the river
merrily merrily swept along
happy to flow where we belong
until we are cast out, rejected,
obstacles we'd not expected,
unreasonable, unclever.

Who am I?
Ask it again.
The first answer is not enough,
mask of clan and name.
Now to discover another truth,
a pattern that is our own.

But when we forsake the binders and markers
we are merged into the whole
with no definition from within
we grasp at any margin
that frames us visible.

Those who love us challenge us,
who do not wish to let us change,
who want us as we were. A stranger
will beckon. We follow.

You are on a quest to find
the thread you only can unwind
within the mazes of the mind
that weaves the pattern for you.

The child must follow the mother, then wait
for her to catch up. She cannot.
The child has run ahead.
The mother is left behind to watch
as colour and shape slowly emerge
or flourish and surge
and a new creature is forged
into fulness, and she is glad.

We work, try to make good,
we nurture, give essential food
to release the free form.
You shall not weary. It is well-doing.
The end is never in sight, keep going.
You need not feel alone.

Far away on your life adventure
bravely go, behold the tincture
taking shape, a crystal
to shine and reflect all and one:
love, the love is immortal.

Male and Female

The boy had a trike with a
tip-up truck-type rear. He
needed something to load it
with, that could be emptied out
again, pedalled from A to B.

A pile of dry leaves, windswept
under the open stair, was
just the job. He set to work
hot and happily to armful
the leaves into his container.

A little girl was watching.
She seemed keen to help but
as soon as he dumped a freight
of leaves into the truck she
swooshed them out again.

He tried to explain: the object
was to move the leaves, to
carry them from where they lay,
by means of his trike, and tip
them out to make a pile elsewhere.

She didn't understand, or pretended
not to, because she went on
sabotaging his all-important task.
At last, frustrated, he shouted
at her. She recoiled, much hurt.

She had no idea it was more
than a game. Surely leaves
were for leaving? Whereas
he knew their true value as
transport fodder for his truck.

Feathered Hats

Those dauntless women in feathered hats
(those magnificent men in flying machines)—
Mrs Pankhurst smuggled onto the stage
in a laundry basket. The idea is from Saul/St Paul,
who loved to brave the crowds but
dreaded women speakers. Barbed wire was hidden
in the flowers along the platform.
It did not hold back the Glasgow police.

"The riddle of Samson," said Agnes Walker,
"means sweetness comes from strength.
Weakness is far from sweet.
Let us swarm like bees in the carcase of the lion."
And *Bluebell*, Flora Drummond, five feet high,
was a *match* for any parliamentary man
as she flaunted the thistle and marched along the Strand.
Janie Allan gave her fortune, others gave their freedom.
Servant girls were tortured, intellectuals spurned.

Why are we so timid today?
One blow to our pride and we knuckle under.
Where is the wire among the flowers?
Where is the sting among the honey?
Where the feathered hats?

Ducks and Bricks

Ducks on this side bricks on that
yin and yang and hot and cold
balanced across the shoulder-yoke:
so to market in China.

Ducks a-swimming, ducks a-diving
ducks a-flying, ducks a-dying
I duck, you duck, we duck—out
out for a duck's egg.

Ducks and drakes play
ugly ducklings, roasted duckling
be a duck then
not a quack
float a canard
drop a brick
be a brick
red brick.

Bricks and mortar, without straw
half-baked, hard-baked
in with the bricks
brickbats
canards.

Ducks on this side, bricks on that
it balances, the Tao.

Black Seas

Till all the seas run black
thick with oil
sludge with oil and
clog to death with oil
cormorants and gulls
their livid staring eyes
and beaks that turn to preen
and taste their own slow-choking death.

Till along the coast
in swarms the fish will die
and all that lives on fish
a burning sea
a searing land
a poisoned world
by the hate we humans never fail
to foster till we choke
as we preen our blackened feathers.

The Alumbrados
(Illuminists, lit by inner light, in 16th century Spain)

The astronauts perceived a city of light
spead over the desert of Western Australia.

The Professor of Poetry scoffed
that such stories should be perpetrated.

His mind was well-schooled to exclude
light in any form, or a city

visible from the moon, built-by ancient
tribes, *alumbrados* of the desert.

Some have survived the raw, white civilisers
and light still dreams in them for us all.

The Page Turner

The long-faced girl has draped herself in a shawl,
whose fringes fall forward when she leans to see
the music on the piano.

She does not play the piano, only reads the music while another
plays: a man whose eyes plead and roll, whose head is bent to
hear, whose mouth moves and fingers touch the keys.

She watches as hands translate notes into sound
devouring the pages so she knows exactly when to stand and take
the tip of the sheet in her fingers to turn it deftly over
before she seats herself again with a glide as if she
has never risen and resumes her motionless vigil
beside the virtuoso.

There is no musical term for this page-turning mechanism:
its eyes can read, its hands are neat, its body does not move
until, precisely and repeatedly, the task is enacted.

The long-faced girl reserves her talents. She keeps
her skills aside. She clothes herself in passivity.
Even the music passes her by, escapes from her turn
by turn and off each page.

The performer ends with ralentando and
applause is joined with a crescendo.
She gathers her skirts and follows him out of room.

Song

"I'll take my sorrow straight"
sings the country girl
steeled with the pride
of strong silent men.

No watering down
no sugar lump in throat
no pain-killing help
to explain it away.

No why's and wherefore's
or blaming it on others
on treatment in childhood
or unfair dealing.

It is straight sorrow.
It is plain pain.
It won't go away
and time does not heal.

I'll be straight with my sorrow
and not turn it aside.
"That's neat, that's neat"
I would not have it other.

Don't make excuses
or ask me to forgive.
Just keep riding on
with your spurs that jangle.

No medicine's bitter drops
No drowning in drugs
No cocktail mixed with pity:
I'll take my sorrow straight.

A Scene for Yourself

Dear, beautiful, middle-aged woman
friend, what can I say?
At the party words were brave,
faces smiled, but
with children leaving home
however fitfully
and husbands retiring with
"so much they want to do"
justifications for our existence
swither.

"Develop your own interests"
is all the rage
(as long as they can be laid aside
when anyone else's happen
to make demands.)

I want to scream: Give it up!
Renounce habits and habitat,
compulsive thinking of others.
Purge the toxic "should" and "ought" from your system.
Create a scene for yourself and act it out
with conviction.
Make up your own lines.
Sound and fury can be significant
if they achieve catharsis,
are preferable to the slow drip of unselfishness.

Do nothing, my friend, but live —
whatever that is. Don't try.

Young Men and Older Cars

It is Saturday afternoon
and young men are in the yard
making love to old cars.

Curved and silken with polish
fat little Morris Minors
are teased open and tenderly
given the works.

Beneath each car lies a man
or he bends over with oil and delicate instruments.
He taps here and loosens there
applies himself to every part in turn.

Better dressed and leaner limbed
the Morris Traveller too has a lover.
She leans slightly, needs new tyres,
relaxes to be jacked up
and expose her underside.

Hour after hour the young men
kneel and prostrate themselves
never heeding the grime and cold:
their desire to be back in the womb
but in control.

And the cars give little starts
of pleasure, engines prime
and tremble
at the climax of long tuning.

A Stable Relationship

In a stable relationship one person
is often the horse, the other the owner.

One person is kept in the stable
and taken out only in harness.

The stable door is divided and
allows the horse to look out.

The harness gives freedom of movement
but none of direction or speed.

Horse and owner often enjoy
the deepest trust and intimacy.

But horses have been known
to break out of the stable

and to bolt away, dangling
an end of broken halter.

True Story

I'm going to dance the night away
the dark the tedious faceless hours
I'm going to love my life today
reclaim delays and detours

The dark the tedious faceless hours
when no image carries me
within its passionate desires
and I forget my true story

When no image carries me
into the life I must demand
but I drudge on patiently
in vaguest hope of some reward

Into the life I must demand
I take the hint I take the lead
get up to dance and take the hand
take a turn and find the beat

I take the hint I take the lead
I take the floor I pirouette
I am dancing till I'm dead
my sun arisen image set.

Sacred City

The old makes beautiful what we sense as new
as skyline over High Street and Canongate
    in floodlit outlined shining message
        graces the vision of New Town windows.

The Outlook Tower is white as a candle stem
for Patrick Geddes gave us his sign of hope,
    a look-out post, a lasting beacon,
        humanly making connections earthwise.

This city keeps her principles castle clear
and will not waive them casually with a nod
    to tourist, banker, student, planner,
        visitor, conference speaker, trader.

We live our days in shadow and sidelong sun.
What we attempt is battered by wind and cold.
    The Old Town Geddes touched will slowly
        yield with reserve her warmer closes.

We make our sacred sites by our daily work
and money cannot turn them upsides for profit.
    Neglect may leave their spirit intact
        Flowing anew when discovered quietly.

No need to shout and label and publicise.
No need to claim top prizes or new awards,
    compete and count and measure matter.
        Rather continue in thought and wonder.

On Earth as in Heaven

This poem is a sestina ~ it was inspired
by the book The Hiram Key

What is the secret we must die
to defend? How to build a temple?
Instructions are precise. The rules
are founded, tested, practised, passed on, kept
intact: how to construct a kingdom
balanced on two separate, distinctive pillars.

King and priest: behold the pillars
arched by the keystone of this kingdom:
peace. Peace on earth to be kept
by use of compass, setsquare and rule:
commandments for living: we die
to save the hidden wisdom of this temple.

The stone across the gateway to the temple
is dovetailed on two central pillars
to right and left. These mainstay the kingdom.
Through fear and faith this free way is kept
open to all who undergo the rule.
Choose now to enter: be born or die.

Heaven is earth's sustainable kingdom
where symmetries are ascertained and kept
with measurements exact to reign and rule
until this spirit or that flesh should die
which jointly bear the universal temple:
how do we replace a fallen pillar?

Messages encoded shall be kept
for handing on a tried, enduring rule
or risk collapse. There is one must die
to save the people and rebuild our temple:
upraised a new and visionary pillar
as Morning Star upon our world-kingdom.

Stars conform within their spinning rule.
Sun and moon will set as if to die
but rise again unfailing. We are kept
within the rhythms of this astral temple,
builders with the key to earth's kingdom,
carved in just proportion of each pillar.

Must we yet explode those rules we kept,
compose again the pillars of our kingdom
and die upon the steps of the temple?